YESTERDAY'S ROCHDALE

by

John Cole, B.Lib., A.L.A.

Front Cover: Rochdale Town Centre during 1906 Jubilee Celebrations.

Inside front cover: Rochdale Town Centre in 1850. Scale 60″ mile.

Published by Hendon Publishing Co. Ltd., Hendon Mill, Nelson, Lancashire.
Text © John Cole, 1983
Printed by Fretwell & Brian Ltd., Healey Works, Goulbourne St., Keighley, W. Yorks. BD21 1PZ.

Introduction

In 1086, the town of Rochdale was important enough to warrant a mention in the Domesday Survey (as 'Recedham'), but from then until the latter part of the eighteenth century its growth was peaceful and gradual. Travellers who passed this way described Rochdale variously as, 'a mercate town well frequented' (Camden 1586), 'a pretty neate town built all of stone' (Celia Fiennes, 1698) and 'a good market town of late much improved in the woollen market' (Daniel Defoe, 1724).

The transformation of this stone-built market community into a sprawling industrial centre was sudden and traumatic. Sir James Kay-Shuttleworth, writing in 1893, creates a vivid impression of the effects of such rapid industrialisation.

Where formerly the deer, the moorfowl and the sheep had held for centuries unchallenged possession, mills moved by water power crept up the valleys into their remotest recesses. Scattered hamlets of rude cottages appeared. By and by the huts of quarrymen and coal-miners mingled with the cottages of the handloom weavers and mill hands. Then came the steam engine to displace water power. Domestic labour gave place to the spinning jenny, the water frame and the carding machine. The factories became huge structures. Tall chimnies at their side emitted volumes of smoke in the beautiful ravines worn by the Irwell, the Calder, the Roche, the Darwen and the Ribble. Thus from Burnley to Todmorden through Littleborough, Smallbridge, Rochdale, Heywood, Bury and Radcliffe to Manchester, a chain of towns, teeming with population are strung like beads on the thread of the Roche and Irwell — streams no longer silver but stained purple.

Rochdale, in common with other Lancashire towns, grew without planning or constraint. The expansion of the area far outstripped the powers or abilities of the local officials, an uncoordinated hotch-potch of Justices of the Peace, churchwardens and turnpike trustees, to deal with the accompanying administrative and social problems.

The first attempt to create a more suitable system of local government was the Rochdale Improvement Act of 1825, which defined the town as 'all that area within a ¾ mile radius of the Market Cross,' (at the bottom of Yorkshire Street), established a Board of Commissioners with extremely limited powers — and soon proved to be totally inadequate.

Then, in 1833, the local 'Watching and Lighting Act' placed the feeble old men of the Town Watch (the forerunners of the police force) under the control of a committee of ratepayers. So poor was the service provided by these decrepit watchmen that the committee was constantly at loggerheads with the chief police official — the Deputy Chief Constable. Relations deteriorated to the point where, in June 1835, the committee resolved, 'that in order to prevent further complaints against Mr. Johnson (the Deputy Chief Constable) for not keeping his establishment agreeable, to contract that two beadles be appointed at a salary of 15/- each, weekly — to be deducted out of the Deputy Chief Constable's salary'. William Woolley and William Bentley were duly appointed 'town beadles' and this photograph of William Woolley dating from some time before he relinquished his post in 1841 is (by far) the oldest known photograph taken in the Rochdale area.

Despite a further Improvement Act in 1844, conditions in Rochdale were worsening rapidly. Surrounded by some of the most breathtaking country in Lancashire, the centre of the town was choking with smoke and filth, overcrowded and exceptionally unhealthy. Surprisingly, the outskirts remained relatively unspoiled until the second half of the nineteenth century — as this recently discovered engraving (dated 1850) vividly portrays. Cows graze contentedly on Broadfield slopes and the countryside stretches away to St. Clement's, Spotland (left) and beyond. The building on the right, standing on the site presently occupied by the Broadfield Hotel, is the second Rochdale Grammar School, built in 1847. To its left stands the Holland Street Mill and in the centre of the picture is the old Bankside Woollen Mill. In those days there was no Esplanade, and Manchester Road (seen here complete with cart and carriage) ran straight through to Holland Street.

In 1856, an application was made, at last, for Rochdale to have its own Town Council with all the independence, prestige and civic dignity that went with it, and whilst there was little opposition to the proposal itself, the controversy which arose as to whether Rochdale should be a three or a five ward Borough split the town down the middle and resulted in each faction starting a newspaper to publicize its own point of view. Ironically both the *Rochdale Observer* and the *Rochdale Standard* were united in their strident support of the Liberal Party, so when the dust had finally settled over the 'Incorporation Issue' they had nothing to squabble about and meekly amalgamated as the *Rochdale Observer and Standard*. By 1858 the newspaper had become simply the *Rochdale Observer*.

The Rochdale Standard.

SATURDAY, DECEMBER 20, 1856.

THE MAYOR OF ROCHDALE.

WE congratulate our fellow townsmen, that Jacob Bright, Esq., has been elected to the office of Mayor of Rochdale. The name of "Bright," and the esteem in which the family are held, renders such a mark of honour at once graceful and appropriate It would have been a lasting reproach to the reform interests in Rochdale, if with a decided majority in the council it had been otherwise. In order to complete the council, there now requires only the election of gentlemen to fill the places of those who have been elected aldermen. We trust that the burgesses will in these appointments secure the services of men suited to the office. Want of space prevents us from making any lengthy observations this week upon our future municipal prospects.

MR. PHILLIPS AND THE COMPLETE HISTORY OF THE CORPORATION QUESTION.

"Yes, sir, puffing is of various sorts: the principal are, the puff direct, the puff preliminary, the puff collateral, and the puff collusive, and the puff oblique or puff by implication. These all assume, as circumstances require, the various forms of letter to the editor, occasional anecdote, impartial critique, observation from correspondent, or advertisement from the party "—*Sheridan's Critic.*

THE office of the historian is one that should be discharged with truthfulness, accuracy, and fairness, and when so discharged is worthy of the highest respect, aiming as it does, to teach great truths by the force of great examples.

But the public sense is grossly abused when the writer of a political tirade, full of self-conceit and egotism, and abounding in mistakes both of facts and dates, is allowed to palm off his spurious verbiage under the guise of history. The proper function of such a writer, in Shaksperian language, would be to

—————————— "Suckle fools
And chronicle small beer,"

And truly the small beer chronicled by our contemporary the *Rochdale Observer* last week, was of the most frothy and unwholesome quality.

With what a profound remark he commences,—"An event that is past becomes a matter of history," and how magniloquently he proceeds,—"A record of the doings of those who have figured in the movement generally may serve a useful purpose, and also become a guide for future generations." Such a writer was worthy to have written a history of Little Pedlington.

that further information was needed, particularly as to the cost of obtaining the charter, the expense of working it, and the degree of success which had attended the incorporation of the neighbouring towns. It was at this meeting that deputations were appointed to visit the several towns to obtain the necessary information, and not at the meeting on Aug. 2nd, as stated in the *Observer.* Mr. Cheetham, who knew some one connected with the Ashton corporation, was appointed with Mr. Phillips to visit that place; Mr. Samuel Stott engaged to obtain information from Manchester, Mr. Tweedale and Mr. R. T. Heape offered to get what they could from Halifax and Wakefield; and Mr. W. A. Scott was requested to visit Oldham. All these names are ignored by the writer in the *Observer*, except those of Mr. Phillips and Mr. Cheetham.

On Thursday, the 26th July, Mr. Scott spent the greater portion of the day at Oldham in obtaining such information as was likely to be of use to the town, and gave that information to the meeting of the 2nd August, and a report of which appears in the *Sentinel* of the 4th of the same month. At that meeting Mr. Stott also communicated the information he had obtained from Manchester.

A word or two as to Mr. Phillips's connection with the movement for a charter; at the first meeting, July 18th, he was appointed provisional secretary, but after the second meeting, July 25th, he requested Mr. Scott to relieve him of the duties, and from that time forward took small share in working the cause to its successful issue. He was not named upon the first provisional committee for getting up the requisition to the chief constable, which was composed of the following gentlemen:

Mr. Thomas Ashworth, (chief constable)

Mr. John Mason	Mr. Samuel Stott
,, David Cheetham	,, William Stewart
,, James Petrie	,, Thomas Livsey
,, Joseph H. Moore	,, Richard Berry
,, Joseph Wood	,, W. A. Scott
,, James Tweedale	

We have taken up a large space in exposing the blunders of the writer of the "History of the corporation question," as given in the *Observer* of last Saturday, and have only advanced to the second or third paragraph. We must postpone till next week the discussion of his further inacuracies, — such as that the chief constable *refused* to call the meeting held on the 14th February,—that the gentlemen in favour of five or more wards set on foot a petition in favour of their views before the meeting of the 14th February,—or that the first resolution of the public meeting, 21st September, 1855, was seconded by Mr. Scott, —these are simply mis-statements, got up to give colour to an argument which rests on a basis of misrepresentation from first to last.

The back page of the *Standard*, reproduced here, reports on the election of Rochdale's first mayor and takes the usual hefty swipe at its rival.

One of the most urgent problems facing the new Borough Council was that created by the existence of row upon row of slum houses in the centre of the town. Areas of poverty, misery and pestilence such as the 'Gank', a collection of foul hovels clinging to the slopes bounded by Church Lane and Packer Street, were swept away in a massive clearance programme. In the following series of photographs, we can see how the centre and main shopping streets looked after this first period of reconstruction — and marvel at the equally dramatic changes which have occured since then.

In 1864, the Council advertised for plans for a Town Hall, to cost, when complete, about £20,000. W. H. Crossland put in the successful tender and by 1871 had provided a magnificent building costing, to the fury of a large number of ratepayers, nearly £160,000. On 10th April, 1883, the ornate gothic spire of the Town Hall, which rose to a dizzying 240 feet, was destroyed by a fire. The new tower, a mere 190 feet high, was (in the absence of Mr Crossland) designed by Alfred Waterhouse, the architect of Manchester Town Hall, and was officially opened on 20th June, 1887, to coincide with Queen Victoria's Silver Jubilee.

The photograph was taken in 1893 — prior to the covering of the Roch — from the centre of the old Yorkshire Street Bridge. Beneath the Parish Church, on Town Hall Square, stands Kershaw's Central Corn Mill.

In the mid 1860s, Charles Kershaw married the eldest daughter of Mr G. Brierley, corn miller of Cheetham Street, and before long had become a partner in the concern. He retired briefly, then, in 1886, he established his own business in the Butts. In 1894 he moved to Town Hall Square, taking over, and partially rebuilding, a large cabinet and upholstery workshop formerly belonging to Mr W. Snowden. Charles Kershaw died in 1896, shortly after this photograph was taken, but the business continued to trade under his name for many years. The building was demolished in 1934 amidst a storm of controversy. The proposal to use Town Hall Square as an omnibus station generated such antagonism that for over twelve months the correspondence columns of the *Rochdale Observer* were filled with angry letters from indignant townsfolk. On the left of the photograph are the buildings known as Leyland Chambers.

Taking their name from nearby 'Leyland Brow', Leyland Chambers were for many years the premises of Worth and Worth, Solicitors. J. T. Worth, the senior partner when this photograph was taken in 1900, was high bailiff, registrar of the County Court and clerk to the Market Company. Leyland Chambers disappeared as part of the Town Centre Redevelopment Scheme of 1934.
The buildings which had formerly occupied the vacant land to the left of the Parish Church steps were demolished in 1886. One hundred and twenty-two stone steps lead to the Parish Church and on 12th July, 1759, the churchwardens of St. Chad's noted, 'it is agreed that Thomas Kershaw (sexton) is to have 5/- a year for keeping the church steps clean' — money well earned!

Here, with Leyland Chambers in the background, John Bright surveys his native town. The statue, designed by Hamo Thorneycroft and costing £2,000, was unveiled on 24th October, 1891, and was removed to its present site in Broadfield Park in June 1933 — an action that was greeted with stunned disbelief by the majority of local people. On 7th February, 1935, the magazine *Come to the Fair* immortalized this abduction in verse, to the tune (so they claimed) of 'Cock Robin'.

Who moved John Bright?
Said Councillor Dutton,
"we didn't care a button,
the old chap's dead as mutton
We moved John Bright!"
And the aldermen and councillors showed signs of agitation
When they saw John Bright's new situation.

Who took John Bright?
said Alderman Clark
"We did it after dark
and put him in the park
we took John Bright!"
And the people of the Borough were full of consternation
When they saw John Bright's new elevation.

Returning to the town centre, we can see here the first stage of the river-covering from Yorkshire Street to the old Wellington Bridge, shortly before its completion in July 1904. The second stage, from Yorkshire Street to the west side of Newgate, was opened in July 1910 and the third phase, from Newgate to the present police station approach, was finished in June 1923. On 30th January, 1926, the final stretch, from the Wellington Bridge to Weir Street, was officially opened, thus completing what the *Guinness Book of Records* describes as, 'the widest bridge in the World'.

The photographer, positioned on the Town Hall balcony, has also recorded the old steam tram shed and an impressive row of hansom cabs parked along the Esplanade.

By June 1905, when this photograph was taken, the first section of the river-covering provided 'one of the finest tramway centres in the British Isles'. The floor of the covering consists of 6″ slabs of ferro-concrete laid upon a series of main beams supported by huge ferro-concrete columns. The flooring was paved and the tramway tracks, flagged island platforms and public tram shelters, completed the redevelopment.

At the opposite end of the Esplanade, on Manchester Road, stood the 'Angel'. Together the statue and troughs (one for horses, and one at ground level for dogs) constituted the 'Mackinnon Memorial Fountain', which was presented to the town in 1899 by Miss Ellen Mackinnon, in memory of her late mother, Augusta. The statue, fifteen feet high, was the work of the Imperial Stone Company, East Greenwich and was removed in 1961 due to erosion caused by traffic vibration.

This photograph was taken shortly after the completion of the Queen Victoria Memorial Nursing Home (top right) in 1904. Later to become the Broadfield Hotel, the building stood on the site of the second Rochdale Grammar School (shown in the engraving in the Introduction). Another former school premises stands to its left. This was originally the Parish Church School, which was converted for use as the town's gymnasium in 1897.

Rochdale's main thoroughfare, which follows the ancient packhorse route to Halifax, was originally known as High Street, later as Broad Street and finally as Yorkshire Street. Here, on a typical Rochdale day in 1910, a shrimp seller is pictured outside J. H. King's ironmongers shop on the corner of Lord Street.

This venerable building (now Lloyd's Bank) was formerly the Union Hotel and was used fleetingly, in 1745, by a party of Jacobites — sympathizers of Bonnie Prince Charlie. In front of the building stood the ancient market cross. This was removed as a jest by a band of late eighteenth century delinquents and was discovered many years later underneath a footpath near Goose Lane. The head of the cross is now on display in the Rochdale Museum.

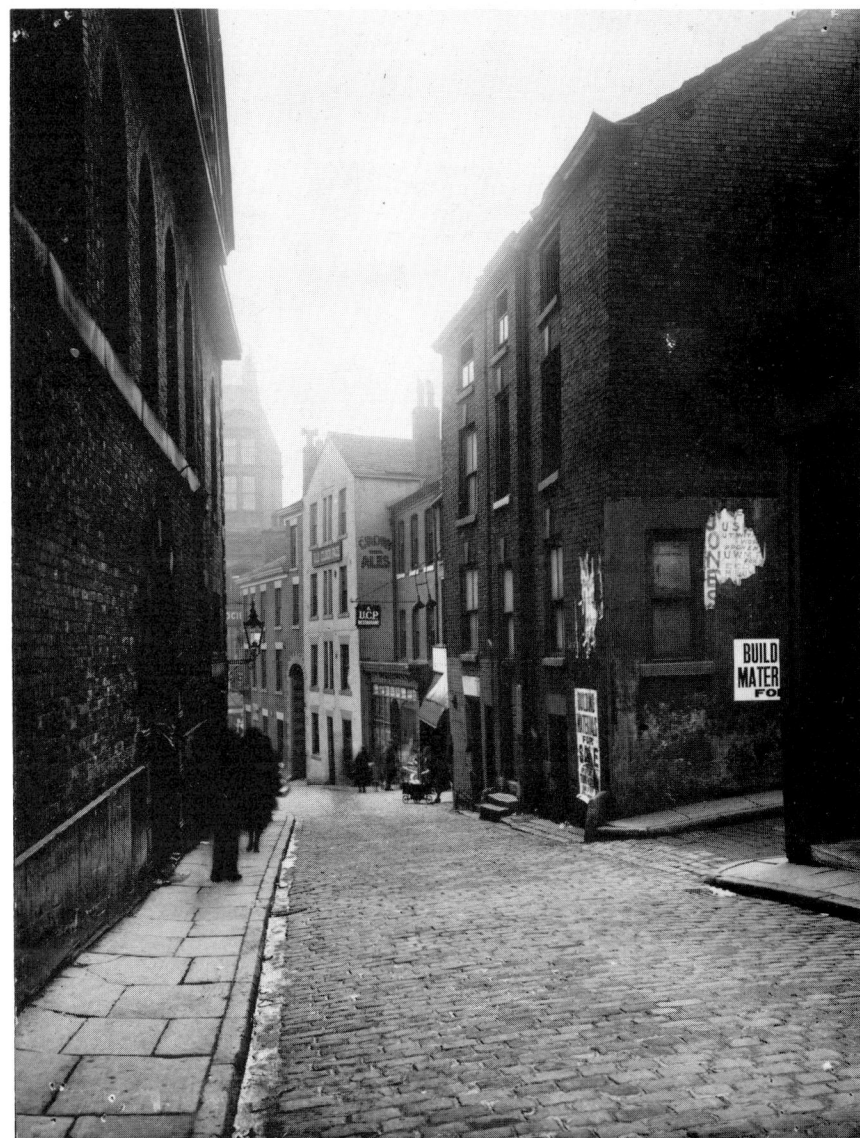

Taken in about 1930, the former premises of J. H. King was by that time occupied by Lloyds Bank Ltd. and where the present Pioneers' Department Store straddles Lord Square, here, Lord Street runs through to the Bishop Blaize Hotel in the distance. Descending the street, on the right hand side, we have: Tweedale's Tobacconists, Henry Rhodes — Tripe Dresser, Hilton's Café, the Lower Market (with the famous combined pillar box and gaslamp, now to be found in the Toad Lane Conservation Area) and the Old Clock Face Hotel standing on the corner of Toad Lane.

Formerly one of the longest streets in Rochdale, Toad Lane (believed by many to be a corruption of 'Th'owd Lane') must now, surely be one of the shortest. For this photograph, taken in 1930, the camera was positioned looking down towards Lord Street, with the Pioneers' store just discernible in the distance. Barrack Yard is first on the right and the small shop next to the Old Clock Face is one of Samuel Irlam's renowned 'tripe and cow's heel' establishments.

Turning back to Yorkshire Street, seen here in about 1910, Bowden's confectioners occupies the premises on the far side of Lord Street. On either side of the Walk are Joseph Hepworth and Sons, and James Duckworth's Ltd., whilst on the left of the picture market stalls can be seen spilling on to the street in front of J. H. King's ubiquitous ironmongers shop.

The stalls stood on the site of the ancient weekly market (founded in 1240) which moved from its original location in or around Church Lane to the bottom of Yorkshire Street in the mid-sixteenth century.

In 1822 an area bounded by Yorkshire Street, Lord Street, Toad Lane and Bladewater Street was developed by a newly created 'Market Company'. However, despite the establishment of this purpose-built market, the small plot of land outside the present Lloyd's Bank continued to be used by street traders for well over a century.

This startling photograph of Yorkshire Street supporting a two-way traffic system was taken in July 1926. The narrowness of Rochdale's main thoroughfare had long been a problem. Indeed, on 24th May, 1897, the Council agreed that the street should be widened 'gradually and systematically' and, by demolishing the old Town Hall Buildings (so-called, but never used as municipal offices) at the corner of Lord Street, it was proposed to make Yorkshire Street 'Sixteen yards wide at its narrowest point'. Obviously even this was totally inadequate to deal with modern traffic conditions and, on 14th August, 1935, the area from Baillie Street to Cheetham Street was restricted to one-way traffic.

Taken in about 1910, this view of Yorkshire Street shows the tramlines sweeping into Cheetham Street on the left. Until comparatively recently, land in this area was owned by Chetham's (Cheetham's) Hospital, hence the derivation of the name, 'Cheetham Street'. The premises on Yorkshire Street were erected in the mid-nineteenth century, prior to which the land on both sides of the road formed part of an extensive nursery and the only building in the immediate vicinity was the old watchman's hut on what is now Union Street.

Rochdale's other main commercial thoroughfare, Drake Street, was formed around 1810 when Dr Drake, the then Vicar of Rochdale, began selling and leasing portions of the Vicarage Estate. This photograph of 1908 shows an electric tram descending from the railway station to the tramway centre on the Esplanade.

In the distance is James Duckworth's Temperance and Commercial Hotel. Here, at the time, a three-course lunch could be purchased for 1s (5p) whilst a six-course dinner cost all of 1s 6d (7½p). A 'Bed and Meat Breakfast including Attendance' would set the overnight visitor back 2s 6d (12½p).

The improvements and alterations throughout the Borough gathered momentum. The arrival of the electric tramway network necessitated the building of a completely new street (called Mellor Street after Rochdale's first Town Clerk — Zachary Mellor) between Bury Road and Spotland Road. This proved to be a complex feat of engineering as the road had to be carried through mill premises and also involved the complete removal of a 60 feet high hillock. The River Spodden had to be bridged twice and the whole operation was hindered by the existence of a rabbit-warren of colliery workings thirty to forty feet below the river. The first photograph shows the site being prepared for the No. 1 Mellor Street Bridge in August 1902.

After the completion of the bridge, in September 1903, the structure was tested by submitting it to as much stress as possible. First of all, a steam traction engine weighing twelve tons and a bogey with a load of eighteen tons were stationed in the centre of the bridge. Another traction engine, of similar weight, later passed over the bridge to simulate the pressure of moving traffic. During these experiments an extremely confident, brave, or foolhardy company of experts was perched on a temporary platform beneath the bridge diligently measuring the stress factors with the aid of deflectors and amplifiers!

As the reconstruction of the town centre progressed, much of the traditional domestic housing in the area disappeared. In September 1863, the Council made their decision to construct their prestigious new Town Hall upon the site known as the 'Wood'. This involved the demolition, not only of the seventeenth century House in the Wood but also Wood Cottage which stood on the easterly end of the area towards Manchester Road. At the time of the photograph (around 1860) the cottage was inhabited by Hugh Taylor, the Superintendent of Rochdale Market, and his wife Margaret, both of whom are pictured here. Prior to that the house was the residence of Joseph Heape, one of the founders of the Baillie Street United Methodist Free Church.

In 1908, Rochdale Corporation cut a new road from Lord Street to the centre of the town. This was named after a small section of the existing thoroughfare — Newgate. In order to accommodate the new road, the oldest secular building in Rochdale, the Great House, or 'Amen Corner' (built in 1585) was demolished. In the same courtyard stood the premises of the Rochdale Tallow and Candle Company and connecting these ancient buildings to the Orchard, or Manor House, was another dilapidated cul-de-sac, Wheelpit Court (pictured here in 1900). In 1921, Wheelpit Court and the Orchard were demolished to make way for the War Memorial, which was unveiled on 26th November, 1922.

Photographs of Victorian domestic interiors are exceptionally rare. Pictured here at tea in their home at 11 Church Stile, are Edmund Fitton and his wife, Hannah. Edmund Fitton was born in a cottage near Dunkirk, Mitchell Hey, in 1821 and for several years was a carpet finisher at John Bright and Brothers'. He was connected with Bury Church until 1861 when he took up the position of choirmaster at St. Chad's, Rochdale. For 30 years he was both clerk and sacristan of the Parish Church. On 18th June, 1895, when he and his wife celebrated their Golden Wedding, the members of the congregation arranged for this splendid photograph to be taken as a token of their appreciation.

The picture is filled with fascinating personal effects and period pieces. On the table, which is set for a tea consisting of toast and butter and huge mugfuls of tea, are Mrs Fitton's knitting, a pair of spectacles, a bible, a copy of the parish magazine and Edmund Fitton's pipe and tobacco pouch. Above the gas lamp is a bell jar and on the range (with its black-leaded surround complete with opened scissors) is a large copper kettle.

While a large amount of domestic housing in Rochdale was of an extremely poor standard, many farms and cottages in the outlying areas were far more sturdily built. Shawmoss Farm, Milnrow, dates from the turn of the nineteenth century and is still standing today, just off Wildhouse Lane. Here, in 1885, Robert Hutchinson, described in the local trade directories as 'a farmer of 18 acres', is pictured in the light suit with the watch and chain. Others in this family gathering include his wife, Susannah (kneeling with the baby), his son, Frederick (far left), his two daughters, two younger sons and an assortment of relatives and neighbours.

Of course, not everyone in the centre of Rochdale lived in inadequate, hastily erected housing. There were, as well, a considerable number of impressive halls and larger domestic buildings. Pictured outside Greenhill, Falinge Road, the residence of Clement Molyneux Royds, is the afore-named's uncle, Albert Hudson Royds. Albert was the eldest son of Rochdale banker, Clement Royds, who became High Sheriff of Lancashire in 1850 and donated the land in Spotland as the site for (appropriately enough) St. Clement's Church. Albert Hudson Royds, born on 11th September, 1811, followed his father into the banking business and also emulated him by building St. Edmund's Church, Falinge, at his own expense. After his father's death, in 1854, he went to live in Worcester, returning to Rochdale in 1880. He was an invalid for many years before his death, on 17th January, 1890.

Slightly more modest was Greenbank, the home of the Bright family. Jacob Bright had arrived in Rochdale from Coventry in 1802, and by 1810 he and a partner had raised enough capital to purchase Greenbank Mill. In that year he and his wife, Martha, moved from their former residence at 28 High Street to Greenbank House, 'a neat country residence situated off Whitworth Road near Cronkeyshaw Common.' Here, on 19th November, 1811, John Bright was born.

The house remained in the family and when this photograph was taken in 1882, it was the residence of John Bright's brother Thomas — who was obviously not averse to the odd game of croquet.

The Brights made a fortune from the textile industry but the meteoric rise of Jacob Bright was by no means unique in nineteenth-century Rochdale. Henry Kelsall, born in Mottram in 1793, was no less successful in adapting to the rapidly changing circumstances. Kelsall moved to Rochdale in 1815 and began a small weaving shop at 48 Packer Street. By 1825 he was able to move into Butts House in the centre of the town and in 1828 he was joined in the business by his brother-in-law, William Bartlemere. In 1856, another brother-in-law, George Tawke Kemp, took over as Kelsall's senior partner and from then on, the business was known as 'Kelsall and Kemp's'. Henry Kelsall died in December 1869, by which time the Butts Mill and Bowling Green complex was well established. George Tawke Kemp's son, George Kemp, was created a baron on 1st January, 1913, taking the title Lord Rochdale.

The photograph shows Butts House (demolished in 1892) and Kelsall and Kemp's Butts Mill and was taken prior to the demolition of the old Wellington footbridge (right) in 1884.

'Cotton was King and his loyal subjects paid daily homage'. This late nineteenth-century weaving shed was equipped with 'Hattersley's Patent Double Action Dobbies' which controlled the raising of the warp threads to provide a varied pattern in the cloth. Each operative would have run at least two looms.

Behind the female operatives are two 'little piecers' — possibly half-timers. Half-timers alternated mornings and afternoons at the mill with attendance at school. Morning shifts were from 6.30 until 12.30 with school in the afternoons; the following week it was school in the mornings and work from 1.30 until 5.30 p.m.

In 1891, Joseph Smalley, Edmund Tweedale and Samuel Tweedale entered into a partnership to build and run a textile machinery manufactory in Castleton. The concern began operating in the following year and, by the outbreak of World War I, had established a considerable reputation in the field. Surprisingly, it was not until the Spring of 1915, (when the need for the acceleration and re-organization of the munitions supply became desperate) that it was realized what a useful contribution textile machinists and machine-tool makers could make towards the war-effort. The Munitions of War Act of July 1915 placed selected companies on something approaching financial parity, as compared to open competition in peacetime, and took them over as 'Controlled Establishments'. Wages were fixed, industrial action was forbidden and for the next three years, as the photograph vividly portrays, Tweedales and Smalleys turned out huge quantities of bombs, shells and grenades.

Next to agriculture and the early textile trade, coalmining, which began here in an organized way in the mid-sixteenth century, was the oldest established local industry. The workings were numerous, if, on the whole, fairly modest in size, and the wealth which could be extracted from these seams is attested to by the lengthy and bitter disputes over mineral rights, which dragged on interminably throughout the eighteenth and nineteenth centuries. The largest colliery in the area was that at Butterworth Hall, Milnrow (pictured here in about 1910), which began operating in the mid-nineteenth century producing low-grade coking coal. The concern was acquired by the Platt Brothers in the 1880s but by 1936 the seams were largely worked out and the colliery was taken over by Oldham Corporation — the underground network of streams providing a supplement to Oldham's water supply.

There were, of course, excellent opportunities in industrial Rochdale for the family concern and the small businessman. The quality of Dixon's soap products was undoubtedly of the highest, but it was the dramatic disappearance of the works in Canal Street which tended to linger in the public memory. A fire broke out shortly after 7 p.m. on 9th November, 1923, and by 8.15 the interior was 'like the glowing crater of a volcano in action'. Damage was estimated at £15,000.

Here, in happier circumstances, in 1892, the cart loaded with sacks and boxes of 'Dixons's Rock Soap' pauses outside the Prince Albert Public House.

In the 1880s, the demand for cheap clothing increased dramatically. Consequently wages in the tailoring trade were kept low as the processes involved became more and more subdivided. Instead of one individual producing a complete item, there were tailors who only made coats, those who specialized in waistcoats and others who produced trousers. In the tiny rooms of private houses, sometimes no more than nine or ten feet square, lighted by naked gas jets and heated by suffocating coke-burning stoves, up to half a dozen men worked day and night. The sweatshop seen here, which belonged to Tom Whitworth (with the hat), was situated on Hurst Street and the photograph dates from some time before the business moved to new premises on Oldham Road around 1900.

The development of the internal combustion engine brought new opportunities for local entrepreneurs — a fact soon recognised by Alfred Stott, seen standing here (with friend) outside his shop at 393 Manchester Road. From these premises Mr Stott supplemented his income by selling gramophone records and providing a taxi-cab service. When he moved to
18 Lord Street, in the 1930s, the site was acquired initially by John Ainsworth's, printers, but was subsequently developed by Clarke's Motors Ltd.

Whilst local businessmen flourished, the Corporation continued to struggle with the pressing social problems caused by massive industrialisation. One of the most underdeveloped aspects of local government provision was public health, particularly in those areas of waste disposal and sewage purification. Typhus was rampant and, even in the early 1860s, thousands of the town's middens were left for months before being emptied. By 1869, however, thanks largely to the efforts of one man, Councillor Edward Taylor, the 'Rochdale System of Night Soil Disposal' was in operation. Ten-gallon tubs of deodorized waste matter were collected and taken by cart to the treatment works on Entwisle Road and the photograph, dating from the year 1870, shows the collection van approaching the gates of the treatment plant.

Accommodation for the sick was a continuing problem for the authorities. In 1878, the Corporation found itself in desperate need of an isolation hospital and as the old Marland Workhouse (built in 1864, but discontinued in 1877 upon the completion of the Union Workhouse at Dearnley) possessed a small infirmary, they were forced to rent this section of the building as temporary accommodation. In 1886, the Corporation finally purchased the Workhouse and reconstructed the premises to provide 56 beds, a separate administrative unit, a hand laundry and a mortuary. The photograph dates, in all probability, from the transitional period between 1878 and 1886.

One of the other major responsibilities of the local authority was the provision of an efficient fire service. The original fire station was situated on Smith Street and horses were frequently hired from stables at the rear of the Wellington Hotel. On 10th June, 1893, the premises on Alfred Street were officially opened and fire appliances in 1905, when this photograph was taken, included one horse tender, a dogcart escape and a horse ambulance, each fitted with a special swinging harness. Six horses were kept at the rear of the engine house and the doors of the station were equipped with a novel device which caused the halter ropes to fall from the horses' necks as the main doors swung open.

As Rochdale grew in size, council workmen could be seen industriously digging, paving and laying pipes throughout the Borough. The main sewerage operation undertaken in 1899 was the construction of the intercepting sewer for the Stanney Brook Valley — along Belfield Lane and Newbold Street. The work, shown here in progress in November 1899, was not completed without incident. A claim for surface damage was made by John Hutchinson of Newbold Street, whose property stood above some of the excavations.

Increased traffic using the Milnrow–Rochdale Road, and attempting to cross over the canal bridge at Firgrove, caused tail-backs comparable with the worst of today's urban snarl-ups. The old stone bridge which was no more than 13 feet wide was replaced by a ferro-concrete structure over 14 yards wide and costing nearly £3,000. The photograph, showing the pipework, the frames and the construction was taken on 10th July, 1906.

Other nearby authorities were also making great strides in the provision of public facilities. On 4th July, 1908, Milnrow Library was officially opened by Councillor E. G. Lamb, J.P., the chairman of the District Council. The premises, which cost £2,587, were built 'at the expense of Mr Andrew Carnegie, the millionaire laird of Skibo Castle, Scotland', who had been approached with a proposal to build a library in Milnrow in 1902. The furniture was of 'fumed oak' and the library could boast 'a spacious borrowers' hall, and lending library, a general reading room, a ladies' room and boys' room'.

Since the foundation of the Rochdale Grammar School by Archbishop Parker in 1565, the town of Rochdale has always been in the forefront of educational provision. In 1888, the Technical School Committee obtained the use of rooms in the Town Hall for the new School of Art. The new Technical School premises (now Broadfield Upper School) opened on 26th April, 1893, and the Art School transferred there on 29th April, 1908. The photograph of the Life class in the new building dates from the year 1909.

The 'Laundry Class' in the Technical School is pictured here in 1901, when the teacher was Miss Stanley, and classes were held from 7.00 p.m. until 9.00 p.m. on Tuesday evenings. The course embraced 'instruction in the best method of washing, starching and ironing.'

The expansion of Rochdale would not have been nearly so marked without the development of a sophisticated network of transport and communications. The state of local roads, despite a series of Turnpike Acts beginning in 1734, was generally, appalling. After many years of agitation the first Rochdale Canal Act was passed in 1794 and ten years later the canal was open throughout, from Manchester to Sowerby Bridge in Yorkshire. Notwithstanding the advent of the railways in the 1840s, the canal prospered throughout the nineteenth century. However, by the early twentieth century, commercial traffic was declining and the canal was used increasingly as a leisure facility. Here, on 27th July, 1907, the Juvenile Rechabites (the junior division of the temperance organization known as 'The Independent Order of Rechabites') pass under Ben Healey Bridge, Littleborough. The building on the right of the picture is, rather ironically, the Railway Inn.

Many years after the opening of the Manchester–Leeds Railway, in 1841, the Lancashire and Yorkshire Railway Company somewhat reluctantly resolved to construct a branch line from Rochdale to Bacup. A splendid viaduct of local stone was built to carry the line, at a height of 105 feet, over the thickly-wooded Healey Dell. The Viaduct, which is seen here under construction in 1867, was an impressive feat of engineering consisting of eight arches, each with a span of 30 feet. The figure in the foreground is one of the workmen employed on the viaduct and not the least remarkable feature of a remarkable photograph is the dry river bed — indicating that the Spodden was temporarily diverted whilst the work was in progress.

The original Rochdale station (which opened in 1839) was situated off Oldham Road near the present goods yard and its immediate successor, built in the same locality, was described as 'a curious combination of timber, stone and brick, shabby, mean and comfortless without a single redeeming feature.' In 1889 this was replaced by a brand new building approached via Maclure Road and sited 300 yards further along the line towards Manchester. These premises (pictured here in 1910) were a great success, possessing two long island platforms and an 'umbrella roof' which had the *Rochdale Times* groping for superlatives: 'This resembles a curiously contrived piece of net work or a cunningly wrought spider's web . . . the passenger is in danger of going into an absolute rapture of delight.'

The station steps, seen here in 1906, were described in the *Engineer* magazine of August 1889.

The entrance hall is 36 feet long and 30 feet wide with a high roof of slim iron and plenty of glass; it is so splendidly lighted that one can read in it with pleasure. On the left is the booking office and to the right, the parcels and left luggage office. The short and easy staircase, with its ornamental handrails from the booking office to the platforms is twenty feet wide, the lower part of the walls being of chocolate and grey glazed, and the upper part of white glazed, bricks. On either side of the platform buildings is a conspicuous clock some three feet wide.

On the night of 18th March, 1915, a blizzard, which had raged for nineteen hours continuously, reached its peak and, in spite of these conditions, the Leeds–Fleetwood express was steaming through the snow at a steady 40 mph in an attempt to make up lost time. Visibility was down to a few yards when the express cannoned into the back of a stationary stock train on the up-line to Manchester, at Smithybridge. The engine jumped the tracks, the tender tumbled down an embankment, three passengers were killed, and the driver, who was trapped under the wreckage for six hours, died two days later in Birch Hill Hospital.

Naturally, the iron horse did not completely supplant its four-legged rival. Here, William Tatham, local textile machine manufacturer (in the riding boots), is pictured outside his stables at Broadfield, Sparrow Hill, in the late 1860s. He and his daughter, Ann Ellen (on the right), are about to depart on a trip to Manchester. His other daughter, Sarah Jane, is seated on the grass bank. The names of the two servants are not recorded.

Roberts and Co. Ltd. started ominbus services between the Spread Eagle Inn, Cheetham Street, Rochdale and the George and Dragon Inn, Bacup, in the late 1860s. William Roberts, who originally operated from Pippin Bank, Bacup, was one of the many carriers who used the Spread Eagle as a staging post. Others included Joseph Emerson, who ran a service to Bury, George Grindrod, who operated a daily service to Littleborough, and Stockton and Fielding Ltd., who provided omnibuses to Manchester. This particular photograph dates from around 1905.

Over the setts of the old Yorkshire Street Bridge pass this splendid horse and carriage. The year is 1895 and, in the background, just visible in front of the Wellington Hotel, the future, in the shape of two snorting steam trams, is about to make its presence felt.

Rochdale's tramway network, originally operated by the notoriously inefficient Manchester, Bury, Rochdale and Oldham Steam Tramway Company, was inaugurated on 7th May, 1883. In 1899, Rochdale Corporation applied to Parliament for permission to construct and operate an electric tramway system along all the routes already run by the Tramway Company. However, a lengthy arbitration process over compensation resulted in the Corporation constructing several new routes, totally unconnected with the steam tramway network. The second such section to be opened (with all due ceremony on a typical spring morning — 22nd May, 1902) was the line from Dane Street to Bury Road.

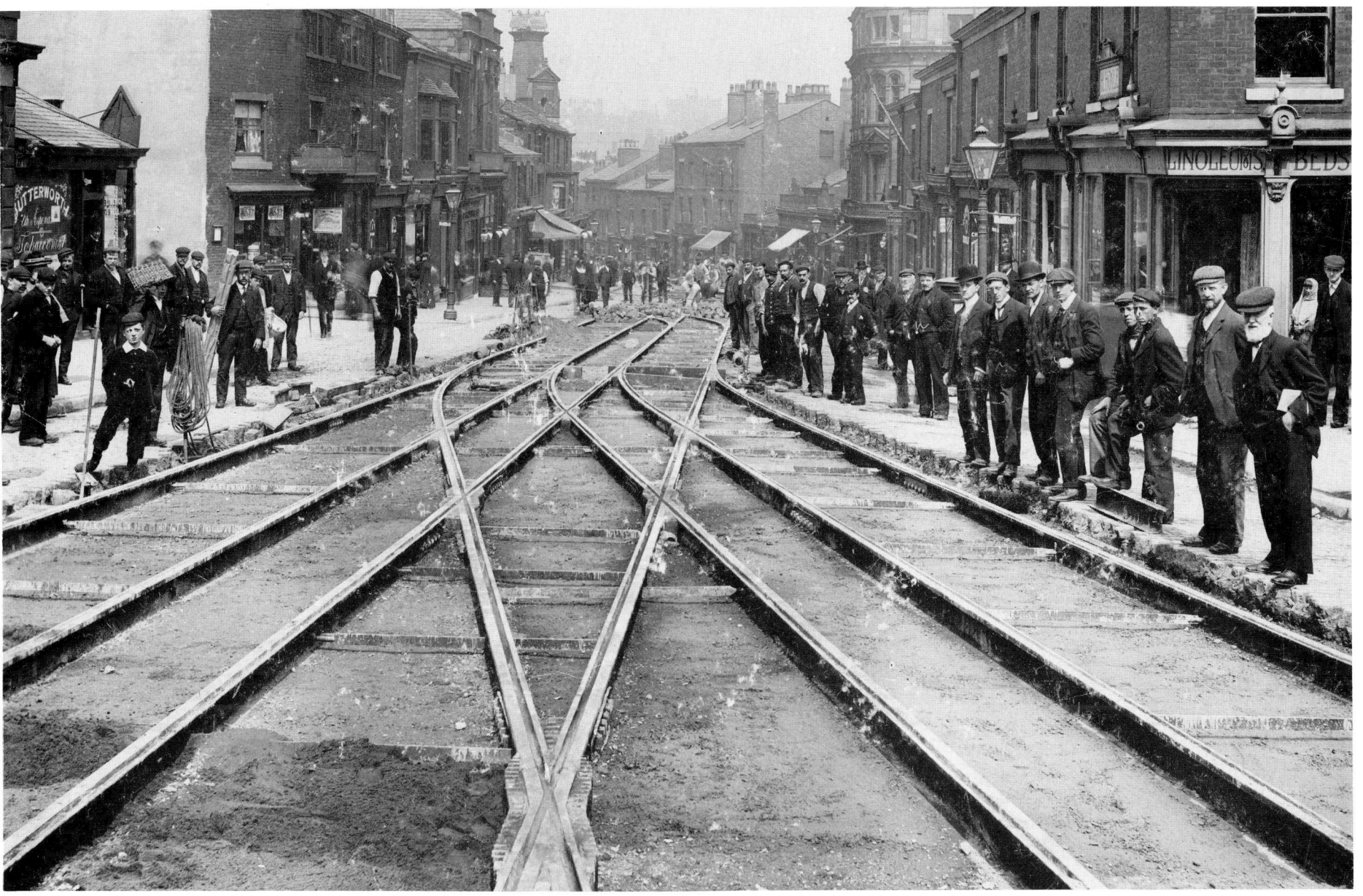

In April 1904, the old steam tramway lines on Drake Street were dug up in order to accommodate the tracks for the new electrified circular route connecting the railway station with the town centre. This section began at the Town Hall, continued along South Parade, up Drake Street to Oldham Road, then along Oldham Road to High Level Road and Rochdale Station. From there it passed through Tweedale Street, down Manchester Road, and along the Esplanade to the Butts. The laying of the track (pictured here) took place in June 1904 and the line was officially opened on 17th August in the same year.

The Mellor Street tram depot, shown here, was brought into use on 15th July, 1904. The shed, 216 feet long by 100 feet wide, had an entrance at either end and was originally designed to accommodate 56 cars. Also in the photograph are the Corporation water car, an unnumbered water tank vehicle with spraying gear at either end, and a four-wheel hopper waggon with a sprinkler attachment for distributing salt in wintry conditions.

As early as 1897 Samuel Underwood of Smithybridge invested in what was probably the first motor car in the district. This is believed to be the vehicle described in the *Rochdale Observer* on 6th March of that year: 'On Thursday last, a horseless wagonette, the first seen in Rochdale, passed up Drake Street. The vehicle, moving gracefully along was an object of much attention. It moved at a good horse's pace.'

The spiritual needs of the inhabitants were catered for by a wide variety of religious establishments, the earliest of which was the Parish Church of St. Chad's, or 'Old Church'. Geoffrey of Whalley was the first recorded vicar of the church, in 1192, but it is entirely likely that an earlier, possibly Saxon, church stood upon the site. Restoration work during the nineteenth century resulted in an almost complete transformation of the building and in the major alterations of the 1870s and 1880s, the porch was replaced, the tower was heightened (and the clock removed) and the chancel was rebuilt and extended. The two photographs reproduced here reveal how the older perpendicular style was replaced by a far more ornate mock-gothic design. The first dates from the mid 1860s and the second was taken from the Vicarage gardens in 1893.

Milnrow's original church was a wooden chantry chapel built at Butterworth Hall in around 1400. The second building was constructed in 1496 and was located on the site now occupied by Nos. 2, 4 and 6 Bridge Street. In 1814, the third Milnrow church, which had originally been erected in 1798, in the south-eastern position of the present churchyard, was razed to the ground and rebuilt. This is the building shown in the photograph. After a long period of frustration and delay the present St. James' Church was finally consecrated on 21st August, 1869, and the old building was demolished shortly afterwards.

Of the many other denominations which flourished in Rochdale, perhaps the most individual-looking building belonged to the Countess of Huntingdon's Connexion. This was St. Stephen's Church in Ball Street, built in 1811 and described at the time as 'substantial though unattractive'. Substantial it certainly was, accommodating 1,000 of the followers of Selina Hastings, Lady Huntingdon (who had founded her sect by seceding from the Established Church in the mid-eighteenth century), and whilst the premises were unusual rather than beautiful, the church was a familiar landmark in nineteenth-century Rochdale. In 1871, about the time of this photograph, the minister was Revd Ebenezer Charles Lewis.

The Methodists were, of course, well represented in the area. In Wardle, the links with Methodism stretch back almost to the foundation of the movement itself. John Leach, the renowned hymn writer was born in the village in 1736 and ordained as a minister in 1773. Prior to the opening of their first chapel in 1809, local Methodists met in the Spring Gardens Inn, Wardle Fold. The present chapel was opened on 8th April, 1874, and the Home Mission caravan was a familiar sight on the village square at the turn of the century. The caravan also visited other chapels in the circuit including those at Littleborough, Milnrow and Whitworth.

Leisure time in the nineteenth century was restricted by the long hours worked in the factory and tended very much to revolve around the streets and the public houses. The Royds Arms on Rooley Moor Road, pictured here in 1871 with licensee Edmund Nuttall and client (on horseback) in the courtyard, was the subject of a less than complimentary assessment in an official report published by the Rochdale Police Department in 1910. This revealed that, in those days, the hotel consisted of a taproom, kitchen and snug downstairs and a club and private accommodation upstairs. There was also a back entrance on Spod Road. The report concludes: 'Internal communication by snug window to wooden hut used as barbers' shop. Snug objectionable.'

One of the most unusual public houses in Lancashire was Uncle Tom's Cabin, popularly referred to as the Boat Inn, at Hamer Lane, Belfield. At the dawn of the railway age, the nearest station to Heywood was at Blue Pits, Castleton. From there, passengers were conveyed to Heywood by canal boat. Finally Heywood acquired its own station and, in 1841, one of the canal barges was hauled on to dry land and transported to Belfield, where it was converted into a small roadside inn. Standing on an even keel, the deck was originally open to the elements and on summer days drinks were brought up from below. However, because dry summer days are the exception rather than the rule, the barge was eventually roofed and the sides built up with bricks. Nevertheless, the slope of the sides and the porthole windows helped to preserve a certain nautical air. Uncle Tom's Cabin was deprived of its licence in 1909 and broken up in the same year.

This photograph is of interest, not only for the motley gathering outside the pub, but also because of its setting. Watergrove Village was a self-contained moorland hamlet, just to the north of Wardle, consisting of a Wesleyan Methodist Chapel, a cotton mill, the Orchard Inn, farms, shops and domestic housing. The Orchard was the recreational, if not the intellectual, centre of the village and here, in around 1910, members of the group loosely known as the 'Watergrove Gun Club' are about to depart for an afternoon's 'sport'.

In 1935 Watergrove Reservoir was officially opened and what was left of the village, along with Roads Mill, Alderbank Mill and Bowers Row, was submerged beneath 720 million gallons of water.

Somewhat of an institution around the inns and taverns of Rochdale was Mick Needham. Described variously as an 'idle fellow' and 'brimful of fun', Needham was usually to be seen dressed in oddments of military uniform energetically drilling eager groups of local schoolchildren, or swaying up Yorkshire Street cadging beer money from passers-by. As the *Rochdale Observer* reported in a short obituary in May 1892: 'A low buzz of a whistle, a sharp salute and your way was blocked by Mick standing rigid as a sentry. Next came a sly hint that a copper would be acceptable.' According to the *Observer,* these tactics were usually successful.

As leisure-time expanded, theatres, clubs, societies and later, cinemas proliferated. On 27th November, 1909, the Palace Roller Skating Rink, situated on High Level Road, was officially opened. The concept of leisure complexes being nothing particularly new, cinema magnates J. F. Moore and Monty Beaudyn chose the site next door to the rink for their latest picture-house, the Coliseum. This was opened in 1911 and boasted a seating capacity of over 1,400. In those days, as the photograph indicates, a visit to the cinema was somewhat cheaper than today! The picture was taken on 10th July, 1913, and shows the staff of the Coliseum about to depart on a charabanc outing.

Because of the restricted opportunities for leisure, events of local or national significance were celebrated with tremendous enthusiasm. On 20th June, 1897, the town greeted Queen Victoria's Diamond Jubilee with an unbridled outpouring of emotion. All the main streets were gaily decorated with lights and bunting and the balcony of the library was draped in cloth of royal blue with yellow fringes.

The photograph is of particular interest because, in addition to showing the library prior to the construction of the Art Gallery extension in 1903, it gives us a vivid reminder of just how many mills existed in the area in the days when 'Britain's bread hung by Lancashire's thread.'

By 10.30 a.m. on 20th May, 1910, 3,000 people had assembled in the Town Hall Square for a requiem service for the late King, Edward VII, who had died a fortnight previously. At one o'clock, more than twenty memorial services took place in the town and to the sombre accompaniment of the Death March, the civic procession, led by the police band, left the Town Hall and marched via South Parade, Drake Street and Church Stile, to the Parish Church where the official service was held.

As we have seen, the Incorporation of Rochdale as a municipal borough had a profound effect both upon the physical appearance of the town and upon the health and well-being of its inhabitants. Consequently, the fiftieth anniversary of this event was marked by a series of special events throughout the Borough, culminating, on 9th September, 1906, in 'the largest and most impressive procession ever witnessed in the area.' Spectators crammed into the narrow streets, hung precariously from windows and balconies and clung like limpets to lamp-posts and telegraph poles. By popular consensus, the greatest attraction was the rushcart. The pyramid of rushes (gathered during the previous week on Blackstone Edge) was constructed in Lowerplace, but because the tradition of rushweaving had died out in the Rochdale area many years before, an expert had to be imported from Crompton to advise upon the correct procedure. The cart was horsedrawn, and was accompanied by thirty Lowerplace men holding the guide-ropes and attired in white shirts, white stockings, light-blue breeches, dark-blue caps and fancy clogs. Also pictured here, as the rushcart proceeds along Tweedale Street, are the Crewe Original Troupe of Morris Dancers.